P. WILLIAMSON

Ferries of Cork

Jack Phelan

CONNACHT

ISBN 1 871947 33 2
Published by

FERRY
Publications

12 Millfields Close, Kilgetty, Pembrokeshire, Wales, UK.
Tel: 01834 813991   Fax: 01834 814484

CONTENTS

Editor: *John Hendy* Design: *Miles Cowsill*

The *Innisfallen* (3) and the *Irish Coast* pictured at Cork. *(Cork Examiner collection)*

INTRODUCTION

What is a *ferry?* When I was a boy at school in Waterford City the word, to me, meant one of the wooden rowing boats operated by the local Corporation across our wide and tidal river. Later it came to mean bigger vessels, still operating on rivers, lakes or estuaries and in my late teens and early twenties, ungainly craft which carried passengers and vehicles across various Scottish firths and lochs.

As used in this publication I have taken the word *ferries* as meaning the ships which in earlier days carried people, livestock and cargo from Cork and since 1969 as vessels running regular services for passengers, with or without vehicles, and for vehicles, with or without drivers and passengers.

Thanks are due to many people for their help in the preparation of *Ferries of Cork*. Miles Cowsill and John Hendy encouraged me to write this study; I am grateful to Cork Harbour Commissioners for their unfailing help over many years and especially to Messrs Sean Geary and Tony O'Leary of the Commissioner's staff for help in research and photographs and to the advertisers who have made this publication possible. On a personal level, special words to my wife Gert for her love and understanding all these years and to my three daughters for putting up with a roving father. The *Cork Examiner* has been generous with ship photos and I am grateful to Anthony Dinan and Lillian Caverley for their help in obtaining these historic prints. I must also mention Philip Booth, who has been my constant travelling companion by train and ship since 1974.

I owe a special debt to my ship mates. John Power and Bill Crofts are, sadly, deceased. Bill Herdman and Michael Hourigan were my seniors for three happy years and my other special sea friends include Richard Egan, John Burford, Timmy Murphy, Martin Foley, Grace Hosford, Anne Farrell and the ladies and gents at Cork, Swansea and Roscoff Ferry Terminals.

Ferries of Cork would not have been possible but for Nicola Phelan who did trojan work on her word-processor.

J A Phelan
November 1995

FOREWORD

by Pat Keenan
Chief Executive, Port of Cork

Pat Keenan

The fortunes of the City of Cork, sitting as it does at the mouth of the River Lee, have, for centuries, been linked inextricably to the wellbeing of the Port of Cork. Today, the City and its environs profit from the ferries which sail in and out of the Port to "feed" the tourism industry in the south west and west of Ireland - the heart of Holiday Ireland.

Over the years, passenger ships have provided the backdrop for joyous as well as poignant scenes. In 1988, we celebrated the 150th Anniversary of the first steam crossing of the Atlantic by the *Sirius* from Passage West in Cork Harbour to New York and the *Sirius*, of course, carried passengers. How many of the forebears of the 40 million or so first and second generation Irish in America today sailed from Cork Harbour following the famine in the 19th century and, more recently, who can forget the joyous scenes which greeted the *Celtic Pride* when she was used by Swansea Cork Ferries to re-open the route linking Cork and Swansea in 1987?

The importance of the ferries to the Port is mirrored in the development of ferry facilities. The change to Ro-Ro ferries saw a move from Penrose Quay in the heart of the City to Tivoli and 1982 marked the move to the new ferryport in Ringaskiddy with the terminal being extended and a second linkspan added in 1995. Today, the Port of Cork - Ireland's Europort - handles almost 400,000 passengers per annum with services to Swansea, Roscoff, St. Malo and Le Havre being provided by Swansea Cork Ferries, Brittany Ferries and Irish Ferries.

Cork and ferry enthusiasts everywhere are fortunate that 'man of ships', Jack Phelan has taken the time and trouble to research this comprehensive history of the *Ferries of Cork*. It is fascinating reading for ship and port people everywhere and will, of course, provide an important reference book for the future.

Pat Keenan
Chief Executive

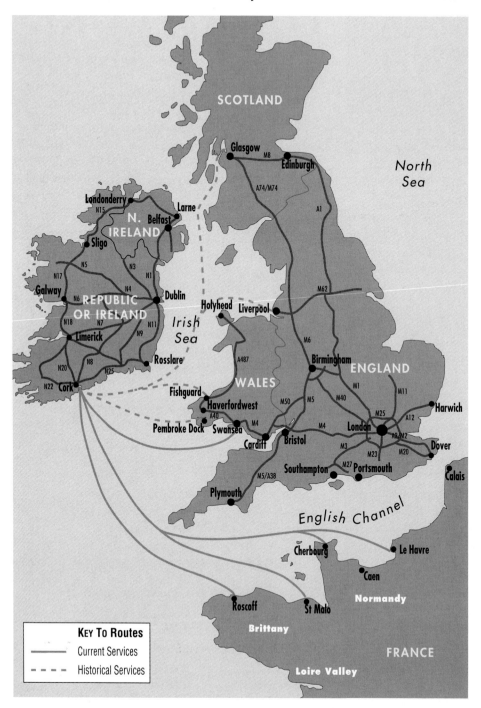

THE CITY & PORT OF CORK

The name *Cork* derives from the Gaelic word *Corcaigh*, meaning marshes. In early times the River Lee, which flows from west to east, spilt into many channels near its entry to a large harbour and many marshes were laid down in the shallows where the tidal waters ceased. Tradition has it that a Celtic Christian saint, Saint Finn Barre founded a monastic seat of learning on high ground just above the marshes and, in due course, Vikings in their longboats arrived and built a settlement, again on the marshes.

Followers loyal to King Henry II came to Ireland in 1169 and in 1185 Prince John gave Cork its first Charter. In the seventeenth and eighteenth centuries the marshes were drained and the City of Cork as we know it took shape.

Cork's port takes in many parts of Cork Harbour. The harbour itself is a wide and sheltered area and stretches from Roche's Point at its southern tip up to Blackrock Castle where the River Lee, having flowed past the City, turns south to reach the sea. The Port really comprises three distinct zones, namely the City and Tivoli docks, the middle region, adjoining Passage West, and the Lower Harbour.

The City Quays comprise North and South Quays, Custom House Quays, (North and South) and some private jetties below the South Quays.

The North Quays are known as Horgan's Quay and Penrose Quay. Horgan's Quay can accommodate large ships but is not used nearly as much as Kennedy Quay and Albert Quay on the South side. Penrose Quay is now largely used by fishing vessels visiting the port at week-ends or in very stormy weather.

North Custom House Quay is in every day use and often sees visiting Naval vessels coming to Cork on courtesy calls. The South Custom House Quay sees little or no commercial activity – it is the usual mooring place for the *Cill Airne*, the former Cork Harbour Commissioners' operated tender for passenger liners at Cobh. The *Cill Airne* now belongs to Cork Regional Technical College and marine trainees (both deck and engine room) make much use of her. The twin Custom House Quays are part of a secure and fenced off complex and public access is restricted. Cork Harbour Commissioners' splendid offices are part of this complex.

The South Quays are in everyday commercial use with ships of all sizes being worked upon. All types of bulk cargoes come and go and the upper port can accommodate ships of 500 feet in length and up to 15,000 tons deadweight.

Immediately at the eastern end of these quays are private jetties which formerly served Dunlop and Ford (now gone); the Electricity Supply Board's Marina generating station has its own jetty where oil and coal discharge plants are situated.

About 2 miles downstream from the City are situated Tivoli Docks. These comprise bulk cargo berths, a large container quay with two container cranes, a roll-on roll-off linkspan and cattle and oil discharge berths. There is an industrial estate adjoining and trade cars are stored and serviced here; there are also chemical, oil and petrol storage tanks and a cattle lairage. Tivoli has the advantage of being rail connected.

In the middle zone the harbour area comprises: Great Island, Fota Island and some smaller islands. On Great Island, at Marino Point, I.F.I.'s fertiliser plant receives many bulkers importing raw materials and exporting the finished product.

Just across the harbour (or West Passage as this particular channel is known), and a little downstream, are Passage West docks where again mini-bulkers and coasters are dealt with. These docks are part of what was once a ship building and repair dockyard and are fenced off from the public.

The Passage West Urban District comprises Passage West, Glenbrook and Monkstown and from Glenbrook a vehicle ferry service operates across the channel to Carrigaloe on Great Island. It is much used and appreciated.

The Lower Harbour area is situated just downstream from Monkstown and offers a rich variety for the ship lover. At Rushbrooke on Great Island, the ship repair yard and dry and floating docks of Cork Dockyard are situated. This facility built many ships but sadly ship building is now a thing of the past.

Just around the corner from Rushbrooke lies Cobh. This town was once known as Queenstown and before that the Cove of Cork. Cobh has a deepwater quay which is now a Cruise Liner Terminal and in the summer season large numbers of cruise vessels are dealt with. These are also smaller jetties in the town and a ferry service operates across the harbour

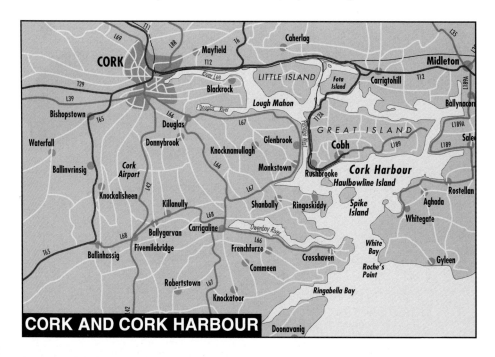

CORK AND CORK HARBOUR

to Haulbowline Island for Irish Steel while a second ferry service is run by the Irish Department of Defence to serve the Naval Base at Haulbowline and the prison on Spike Island. The Pilot Service for Cork Harbour has its own pier at Cobh.

Haulbowline Island was until 1922 the chief base for British Naval Operations in Ireland. A large dockyard was operated there; today the island is partly occupied by Irish Steel Ltd. and they have a quay there where ships bring in raw materials and take out exports of steel bar.

The Irish Navy has its own base on the island from where its seven patrol vessels come and go. Access to Haulbowline Island is severely restricted.

Upstream from Cobh is Ringaskiddy, on the west side of Cork Harbour. Here a deepwater terminal with cranage accepts huge vessels – indeed the *Queen Elizabeth 2* berths at Ringaskiddy once each year – sometimes more. Just above the deepwater quay a chemical factory complex has a single user jetty whilst adjacent to the village of Ringaskiddy is the ferryport terminal for British and Continental vehicle ferries.

Whitegate is situated on the east side of the Harbour and a deepwater jetty here is the place where tankers of up to 90,000 tonnes bring cargoes of crude oil for refining at Whitegate Oil Refinery. Just below Whitegate the harbour suddenly narrows and a passage to the open sea follows with high cliffs on either side. Then this passage opens out slightly and Roche's Point lighthouse on the eastern cliffs marks the entrance to Cork Harbour and the Port of Cork.

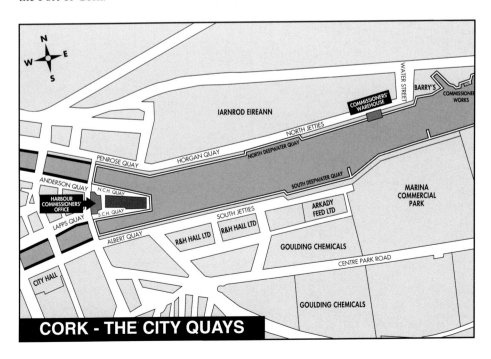

CORK - THE CITY QUAYS

CORK'S FERRY TERMINALS

Penrose Quay near the city centre, and also near the railway stations, was the traditional terminal for passenger ships in the nineteenth century and continued in use until 1968. The St. George Steam Packet Company had its office on the quay and this building became the head office of the City of Cork Steam Packet Company (successors to the St. George Company). The office later served the British and Irish Steam Packet Company Ltd., when the City of Cork S.P.Co. was taken over by the Coast Lines Group at the end of the Great War.

Vessels for Fishguard, Liverpool and Glasgow always berthed at Penrose Quay and the Fishguard service had a special passenger terminal built on the quayside next to the ships.

In 1969 car ferry services moved to the newly built Ferryport at Tivoli. The Tivoli wharves were built on reclaimed land and the car ferries of B & I Line and Brittany Ferries arrived and departed adjacent to a new building which provided facilities for passengers and offices for shore staff attending the ferries together with Customs, Immigration and freight offices. The Tivoli ro/ro berth is still used by freight vessels bringing in trade cars and vans, and the cattle, oil, container and bulk berths are all very busy there. When Tivoli opened it had a fully enclosed walkway for foot passengers using the B & I Line car ferry *Innisfallen*.

Following a decision by Cork Harbour Commissioners to expand facilities in the Lower Harbour, a large area of land was reclaimed in the eighties and a new Ferryport was built at Ringaskiddy about 12 miles from Cork City centre. Brittany Ferries' *Quiberon* was the first user on Saturday 29th May 1982. The terminal had an official opening 12 months later on Saturday 28th May 1983. B & I had previously suspended their service from Cork to

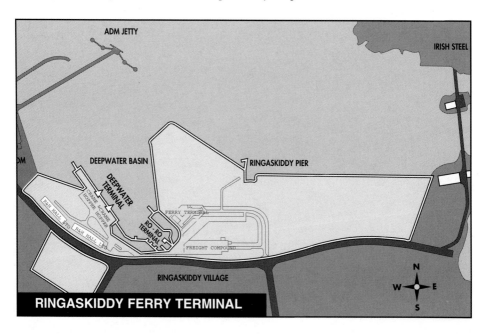

RINGASKIDDY FERRY TERMINAL

Pembroke Dock but did use Ringaskiddy in the summer of 1983 for a seasonal route, again to Pembroke Dock. At the time of writing Brittany Ferries, Swansea-Cork Ferries and Irish Ferries make extensive use of Ringaskiddy where the terminal building was enlarged and renovated in 1994 and a new covered passenger gangway now provides access to all ferries. New areas for motorists have been developed and there is ample car parking for the general public. A second linkspan was provided and has been in operation since March 1995.

Brittany Ferries, Swansea Cork Ferries and Irish Ferries all have service counters at Ringaskiddy Ferry Terminal where bookings may be made on the day if there is space available; these latter facilities are of course only open during certain hours on sailing days. A Bureau de Change operates following the arrival of ferries and prior to departures and there are refreshment, catering and shopping facilities both in the Terminal buildings and the adjoining village. There is also an Information Desk for arriving passengers in the terminal and taxis meet all ferries.

Bus Eireann runs a special bus service from their Cork City Bus Station at Parnell Place for foot passengers departing from Ringaskiddy and they also have a special service to Cork for foot-passengers from arriving ferries. Ringaskiddy is the terminal for a regular bus service from Cork City; this latter service operates via Monkstown and Passage West.

FERRY COMPANY OFFICES IN CORK CITY

Brittany Ferries	42, Grand Parade, Cork	Phone 277801
Irish Ferries	9, Bridge Street, Cork	Phone 504333
Swansea Cork Ferries	52, South Mall, Cork	Phone 271166

The above are all Cork numbers: STD code in Ireland is 021 +
STD code from other countries is + 353 – 21 + local number.

BUS & TRAIN STATIONS IN CORK CITY

Train: Iarnrod Eireann (Irish Rail): Kent Station, Cork

Train Enquiries: Phone 506766
Travel Centre: Phone 504888

Bus: Bus Eireann (Irish Bus): Bus Station, Parnell Place, Cork

Bus Enquiries   Phone 508188

1906 to 1945

The reason for choosing the year 1906 as the starting point for this brief historical chapter is that it was in that year that the Welsh port of Fishguard opened to traffic. As a consequence, the Great Western Railway commenced a new daily service from Fishguard to Rosslare and also made the new port the terminus for its service from Waterford. The City of Cork Steam Packet Company also commenced a Cork to Fishguard service, and the former terminal at New Milford (now Neyland) was abandoned by both companies.

Between 1906 and the start of the Great War, the City of Cork S.P. Co. had two principal passenger vessels. These were both built at Newcastle and were the 1896 built *Innisfallen* (1) and the *Inniscarra* built in 1903. The *Innisfallen* was 272 feet in length whilst the *Inniscarra* measured 281 feet. At 38 feet in width she was two feet wider than the *Innisfallen.*

Whilst these two twin funnelled ships were built within seven years of one another they were dissimilar in appearance . The *Innisfallen* (1,400 gross tons) was the first of five vessels to bear this name. Both were regarded as being well appointed ships and both were lost by enemy action during the war, in May 1918. At that time the *Innisfallen* was working to Liverpool whilst the *Inniscarra* was on the Fishguard route. The *Inniscarra* was torpedoed on 12th May 1918 off the Waterford coast. Only five survived from a total of thirty six people on board. The *Innisfallen* was also torpedoed that month.

The 1914-18 war was disastrous for many Irish shipping companies and the City of Cork S.P. Co. Ltd. suffered greatly. Only two of its ships, the 1893 built *Glengariff* and a collier *Plyades* survived hostilities. With such ship losses the City of Cork S.P. Co. sold out to the Coast Lines Group, which continued the name until 1936. Coast Lines now controlled most of the shipping routes between Britain and Ireland which were not operated by railway companies. The group ran the formerly independent companies as subsidiaries and frequently switched ships from one company to another. Thus ships belonging to the

The *Innisfallen* (1) at the North Quay, seen here on 4th August 1896. *(Dominic Daly collection)*

In 1893, the *Killarney* was built for the Belfast Steamship Company. After a series of name changes, the vessel was purchased by the City of Cork S.P. Co. as the *Classic*. She later reverted to her original name. The vessel is pictured here at Cork. *(Cork Examiner collection)*

British & Irish Steam Packet Company Belfast Steam Ship Company, J. & G. Burns & the Laird Line (all Coast Line Companies) could frequently be seen on Cork services.

A B.& I. S.P. Co. ship the *Kilkenny* reopened the Fishguard service in January 1919, to be replaced the following month by the *Glengariff.*

A third ship arrived to replace the *Glengariff* in July 1919. This ship of 1,500 tons had been ordered by the Scottish firm J. & G. Burns, from A. J. Inglis, shipbuilders of Glasgow and was launched as the *Moorfowl.* Because of a dispute, Burns refused to accept her and she was delivered new to the City of Cork S.P. Co. in July 1919 as the *Killarney.* Her days at Cork were short. She was transferred to J. & G. Burns in July 1920 and resumed the name *Moorfowl.* In 1929 she was renamed *Lairdsmoor* and following a collision in 1937, sank off the Mull of Galloway.

The *Bandon* served for a few months between Cork and Fishguard in 1920. She had been built as the *Louth* in 1894 at Port Glasgow. She continued to serve the City of Cork S.P. Co. until 1931 when she became *Lady Galway* and was transferred to the B & I S.P. Co., finishing her career in 1938.

Due to the troubled state of Ireland two other northern ships ran for short spells with City of Cork S.P. Co. to Fishguard in 1920. They were Laird's *Maple* and Belfast Steam Ship Co.'s *Logic.* They both returned to their owners at the cessation of their charter.

Another change occurred in 1921 when the *Classic* arrived. She had been built in 1893 as the *Magic* for Belfast S.P. Co. She stayed for quite a while becoming the *Killarney* three years after her first arrival. She has a special claim to fame in Irish history. Following the signing of the Anglo-Irish treaty, a Civil War broke out in the Irish Free State and in 1922 at the height of the war the railway between Cork and Dublin was severed and the body of General Michael Collins was brought from Cork to Dublin on board the *Classic.* Collins was Commander in Chief of the newly formed Army of the Irish Free State and had been killed

The *Kenmare* was built for the City of Cork S.P. Co. in 1921. *(William Herdman collection)*

in an ambush by former colleagues in the Irish Republican Army.

In 1931 the *Killarney* (ex *Classic*) was transferred to the ownership of Coast Lines and was converted to a new role as a cruise ship and as such she became a popular vessel operating around the western isles of Scotland. The *Killarney* was finally scrapped in 1948.

In 1929 the management of the Coast Lines Group decided to pioneer new shipping trends when they ordered a new ship the *Ulster Monarch* and specified that she be equipped with diesel engines. Prior to her debut the really fast cross Channel passenger vessels were powered by steam turbines, although there were a number of slower ships with reciprocating steam engines. The Group then had a new *Innisfallen* built at Belfast, a half sister to the *Ulster Monarch*.

She too was given diesel engines and her gross tonnage was 3,019. She was the only passenger motor vessel running to South Wales and proved very popular with Cork/Fishguard passengers.

In 1938 the last British soldiers stationed in Southern Ireland, at Spike Island in Cork Harbour, left on the *Innisfallen*. They were ferried out to her in the Cork Harbour tender *An Saorstat* – a name which translates as the *Free State*.

Liverpool, of course, was still connected with Cork by a passenger and cargo service and Coast Lines had provided a new ship, built in 1921. This was the *Kenmare*, a ship which by virtue of many years faithful service endeared itself to generations of Corkonians. The *Kenmare* and smaller *Ardmore* worked the Liverpool service up to the start of the Second World War.

Right: This picture shows British troops transferring to the *Innisfallen* (2) from the Spike Island tender *An Saorstat.* *(Cork Examiner collection)*

In 1936 Coast Lines, for commercial reasons and following a review of their operations, decided that the B & I Steam Packet Co. Ltd. would assume full ownership and operation of the Cork Services and from that date the Cork ships adopted the livery, flag and funnel colours of B & I. A newly incorporated company the City of Cork Steam Packet Co. [1936] Ltd., became agents of B & I in Cork and surrounding area.

At the start of World War II the situation of Coast Lines Group ships trading to Ireland differed greatly from that which pertained in 1914. Cork ships now flew the Irish tri-colour, and were neutral. For all their neutrality they were trading to belligerent ports and their real owners were Coast Lines, very much non-neutral. Coast Lines switched the *Innisfallen* to Dublin for the Liverpool service and the *Kenmare* was transferred to work cattle and cargo

The **Kenmare** (left) on the Penrose Quay while the **Ardmore** comes astern up to the Liverpool berth. *(William Herdman collection)*

The launch of the *Innisfallen* (2) at Belfastin 1930. *(William Herdman collection)*

only to Fishguard, where she was joined by the *Ardmore*.

In late 1940 a double tragedy occurred. The *Ardmore*, built in 1923 and normally only allowed 12 passengers, sailed from Cork to Fishguard on 11th November and was never seen again. The body of Captain Ford was found near Aberystwyth on 3rd December 1940 and that of Able Seaman Frank O'Shea on 13th December on another Welsh beach. A total of 24 lives were lost and the loss of the *Ardmore* is still a mystery.

Then on 21st December 1940 the *Innisfallen* outward bound from Liverpool to Dublin struck a magnetic mine off the Wirral shore near New Brighton and went down with the loss of 4 lives. No passengers were killed and all 157 of them and the remaining crew were saved.

The *Kenmare* was now the last ship which had been built for the City of Cork Steam Packet Co. She now carried B & I livery and funnel colours and bore the distinguishing marks of a neutral vessel. She kept open the service from Cork to Britain for the remainder of the war, albeit without passengers.

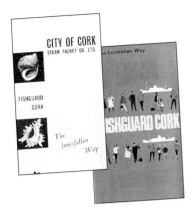

CORK - FISHGUARD
1945 TO 1965

Passenger services from Cork to Fishguard resumed in 1945 following the ending of the war. B & I utilised the *Kenmare* and the pre-war pattern of three times per week, at night in each direction was repeated. The *Kenmare*, which was built in 1921, was by that time rather old and out-dated but she provided a good service.

War losses were now being made good and a new *Munster*, actually built for the B & I Dublin to Liverpool route, replaced the *Kenmare* early in 1948. This new ship ran for a few months before leaving for its intended service. Amazingly the *Munster* built in 1948, withdrawn and sold in 1967, has continued on in the service of Greek owners ever since and first as the *Theseus* and since 1969 as the *Orpheus* has been employed as a cruise ship. The *Orpheus* has been in Dublin, Cork and Waterford in recent years. The *Munster's* gross tonnage was 4,115.

For many years B & I, and its predecessor the City of Cork S. P. Co., had exhorted passengers to "Travel the *Innisfallen* Way". From mid-1948 it was again possible to do just that as B & I introduced to Cork their newly built *Innisfallen* (the third ship to bear this

The *Innisfallen* (2) seen making her way down river from the City of Cork. (*William Herdman collection*)

Fishguard Harbour with the *St Andrew* arriving from Rosslare and the *Innisfallen* (3) seen at the layby berth pending her evening departure to Cork. *(Ferry Publications library)*

name). This handsome and popular ship was a joy to behold . The dark green hull, cream upperworks and the green, white and black funnel introduced a new and fashionable livery on the River Lee and the new ship once again made a mockery of the prophecies that the *Innisfallen* (in Cork dialect *Dinnis*) was too big for the route.

When Fishguard replaced New Milford and Rosslare was opened to supersede Waterford, a new specially constructed Express train, the *Rosslare Express* commenced to run from Cork via Waterford to Rosslare to cater for passengers on the new turbine steamers of the G.W.R. Commercial and business interests felt that with the new facilities introduced by the Great Western Railway and the then Great Southern & Western Railway of Ireland that there was very little need for passenger vessels from either Waterford or Cork. Since 1906 pessimists have claimed that each new building for the Cork direct route would be too large and would accordingly operate at a loss. These pessimists have now been wrong for nearly 90 years.

As before, the service was from Cork on Mondays, Wednesdays and Fridays and from Fishguard on Tuesdays, Thursdays and Saturdays. The ship lay over during the day at Penrose Quay, Cork and at Fishguard and put to sea at nights. A daily service in each direction was still years away and, as in pre-war days, the ship carried livestock and general cargo in addition to its passengers.

In 1948 the *Innisfallen* measured 3,705 gross tons, length 340 feet overall, with a width of 50.2 feet and a speed of 18 knots. She had Denny Brown stabilisers – a great advance on previous ships. From 1952 another of the Coast Line's fine motor vessels came occasionally to the Cork-Fishguard route. This was the *Irish Coast* which relieved the *Innisfallen* when the regular vessel went to dry-dock for its annual overhaul and survey. The *Irish Coast,* launched in Belfast on 8th May 1952, was the second last of the family of thirteen ships constructed for Coast Lines between 1929 and 1957. Its tonnage was 3,813; it was turned out in Coast Lines livery and funnel colours and relieved the regular vessels on all Coast Lines passenger routes between Britain and Ireland. It was sold by Coast Lines in 1968 and saw further service in the Mediterranean.

Meanwhile in 1953, Coast Lines' thinking had undergone a further change, and so once again services from Cork to Fishguard and Liverpool were operated by the City of Cork Steam Packet Co. [1936] Ltd., and the *Innisfallen* was repainted with a black hull with white superstructure and a white funnel with black top (the traditional funnel colour of the City of Cork S.P. Co.) was sported by the Company's ships.

It seemed that nothing would ever change the placid existence of Cork to Fishguard; the pleasant departure time of 6 p.m. from Cork, the lovely progress down river from Penrose Quay, attentive stewards on board, the Captain gracing the 1st class dining room for dinner as the ship sailed towards Fishguard, breakfast in the dining car en route from Fishguard to Paddington, and the daily list of important passengers sailing the *'Innisfallen Way'* published in the **Cork Examiner.** And so the *Innisfallen*, with occasional appearances from *Irish Coast* kept the service going until 1967.

CORK/LIVERPOOL 1948 – 1963

The name *Kenmare* keeps cropping up in the accounts of the Cork-Fishguard and Cork-Liverpool services. It was fitting that when B & I restarted the passenger services from Cork to Liverpool in February 1948, the *Kenmare* was the ship to do it. The *Kenmare* had been built at Ardrossan in 1921.

Apart from saloon and steerage passengers, cattle and general cargo also formed part of the *Kenmare's* manifest.

The *Irish Coast* seen at the berth in the heart of the City of Cork. *(Cork Examiner collection)*

Ferries of Cork

The *Glengariff* was employed on the Cork-Liverpool service until 1963. *(Capt. S. Sydenham collection)*

Having survived the war and operated six nights each week between Cork and Fishguard, the once weekly run to Liverpool was no problem for the *Kenmare*. She sailed from Penrose Quay on Saturdays..

The *Kenmare* had a sister ship – the 1921 built *Ardmore*. This latter ship was sold inside the Group becoming the *Lairdshill* of Burns & Laird in 1930. By a curious co-incidence, or indeed series of co-incidences, the writer made his first ever cross-Channel voyage from Dublin to Greenock on the *Lairdshill* in July 1949 and travelled from Dublin to Glasgow on the *Irish Coast* on his honeymoon in September 1955.

On Saturday 12th May 1956 the *Kenmare* made her last voyage from Cork to Liverpool. The City of Cork S.P. Co. replaced *Kenmare* with the *Glengariff*, of 1,599 tons which had been purchased from the Clyde Shipping Co. of Glasgow. The *Glengariff* was built in 1936 as the *Rathlin*. She was no stranger to Cork having replaced the Clyde Shipping Company's *Fastnet* on the Glasgow-Dublin-Waterford-Cork-Glasgow route in 1950 .

The *Glengariff* had well appointed passenger accommodation but was at first disliked by regular Cork-Liverpool travellers as she had no third class [steerage] accommodation. In the war she became famous as a Convoy Rescue Ship and many sea-farers owed their lives to the tough Clyde built steamer. She was the very last Cork-Liverpool passenger vessel and was disposed of by the City of Cork S.P. Co. in 1963. Thus ended the passenger connection between Liverpool and Cork. Her replacement was the much smaller *Glanmire*, which was a cattle/cargo carrier only. The *Glengariff* and the *Glanmire* were launched on the Clyde and on the Lagan on the same day in 1936 both for Scottish companies.

This view of the *Sanda* shows the vessel leaving Cork for Glasgow.
(Cork Examiner)

CORK/GLASGOW 1945 TO 1952

Cork had a passenger connection to Glasgow for very many years. This was provided by Clyde Shipping Company and although not really a ferry service it briefly deserves mention.

Following the cessation of hostilities in 1945, Clyde Shipping re-established many of its post war services The *Fastnet* resumed a cargo service from Glasgow to Dublin-Waterford-Cork carrying a limited number of cruising passengers. This was a very popular service, but very few ordinary passengers used it as a means of travelling from port to port. The *Fastnet* was sold in April 1950, and replaced by the *Rathlin*. This ship ran until 1952 when it too was sold by her owners. The service then became cargo only operated by the newly built, engines aft, motor vessel *Sanda*. The passenger service ceased on 18th October 1952. The *Sanda* continued to operate until 11th January 1960 when the service finally ended. The *Sanda* then transferred to the Waterford and Liverpool service until her sale to Singapore interests in 1963.

B & I LINE 1965 TO 1983

In February 1965 Coast Lines concluded an agreement with the Irish Government; this document provided for the sale by Coast Lines of its shares in the B & I Steam Packet Co. Ltd., to the Government. Irish interests had been anxious to purchase the B & I for many years; the war had proved that an independent country which was also an island should have some control over shipping and the purchase complemented the deep sea services run by Irish Shipping Ltd.

At first the new ownership made little difference to the Cork-Fishguard service. A new red

The *Innisfallen* (3) dressed overall at Cork. *(Charles Lennon)*

symbol, usually referred to as "the fertility sign" was added to the white funnels of the Cork Ships but the use of the style City of Cork S.P. Co. was immediately discontinued and a new logo B & I Line became the marketing ploy.

Changes were coming though; when the *Innisfallen* went to dry dock and survey she was replaced by the cargo only *Glanmire* and as a result passenger services were suspended during such periods.

Then in 1967 B & I Line announced that new car ferries were on the way and that their three post-war passenger vessels would be disposed of. These ships were out-dated in as much as the growth of road traffic demanded that tourists have transport for their cars. Existing vessels could only crane load very small car numbers.

A new *Innisfallen* was ordered in Germany. She would be a sister to a new *Leinster* being built at Cork for the Dublin-Liverpool route. However a much bigger and more fundamental change was on hand. British Rail gave notice of the termination of the agreement whereby Cork ships could use Fishguard.

B & I Line now arranged for the proposed car ferry service to run into Swansea from Cork. The 1948 *Innisfallen* was sold to Greek interests. Meanwhile since Penrose Quay in the City Centre was manifestly unsuitable as a car ferry terminal, Cork Harbour Commissioners set about the development of new facilities at Tivoli, about 1.5 to 2 miles downstream. Here were constructed a deep water quay with bulk discharge facilities, a container berth, a new cattle berth and lairage and most importantly a linkspan and all associated facilities for a vehicle ferryport including a covered passenger gangway..

New offices with excellent waiting and check-in areas were built and over in Wales a linkspan was built at the mouth of the River Tawe immediately adjoining the locks leading into the King George V and Prince of Wales Docks. Gone were the old, cold waiting rooms built in sheds and railway stations in Cork and Fishguard. Everything was light, bright and up to date.

The new *Innisfallen* duly made her maiden voyage in 1969 and changes all round resulted. Daily services, seven days each week, replaced the old leisurely ways, fast trains from Swansea replaced the long and tiring run from Fishguard, and motorists were now much nearer Britain's developing motorway system.

The fourth *Innisfallen* was herself typical of the age of car ferries; clean, clinical, classless and with a speed of 24.5 knots able to show her stern to anything else on the Irish Sea and St. George's Channel. This speed was specified to enable the ferry to accomplish the return journey every day and still allow sufficient time for the turn around in the ports. It was of course necessary for her to dry-dock annually and normally her replacement was her sister *Leinster*. However a very superior class of ship came in January 1978 to do relief; this was the *Stena Germanica* (5,195 gross tons). The Stena Line ship had many cabins above the car decks, which was a very limited facility on the *Innisfallen* and the *Leinster*, and absent on their smaller first cousin *Munster*. Built for Stena Line in 1967 she could carry 1,300 passengers, 190 cars and her speed of 23 knots made her very suitable for the long sea crossing. Following her Cork stint she was an accommodation ship at Aberdeen for a period prior to sale to Panamannian owners and loss through grounding as the *A. Regina*.

Large volumes of cars and their passengers were experienced in the early years while freight also quickly made the transition from break bulk to ro-ro lorry and so the years passed amidst talk of a second vessel for Swansea-Cork or possibly a dedicated freight ro-ro ship. Indeed B & I Line did have a freight ro-ro vessel *Dundalk* built in 1974 at Cork. Ironically she never ran out of an Irish port for B & I Line and when she did eventually operate on Irish routes it was first as the *Stena Sailer* on charter to Sealink and subsequently as the *St. Cybi* following her purchase by the

The fourth vessel to take the name of *Innisfallen* was built in 1969. This view shows the vessel getting underway for Swansea. *(Jack Phelan)*

This picture shows the *Connacht* in the fitting-out basin of Rushbrooke dockyard shortly after her launch. *(Jack Phelan)*

latter company.

The *Innisfallen's* gross tonnage was 4,848, a huge advance on her earlier name-sake. Even so it became clear as the seventies progressed that B & I Lines' trio was too small, something which applied to all the car ferries between Britain and Ireland. So the ferry of the future was ordered from Verolme at Cork and in 1978 the new *Connacht* was launched. This ship measured 6,812 gross tons; she could carry 350 cars and had greatly superior accommodation for 1,500 passengers. The lesson of the *Stena Germanica* had been learned and a large number of cabins were provided above the car decks.

The *Connacht's* maiden voyage was on 7th February 1979. Prior to her appearing at Swansea she had made promotional appearances in Cork and as far afield as London. Her days at Swansea were few; B & I Line decided to transfer its services from Cork to Pembroke Dock, an old naval base sporting a new ferryport and linkspan. The Company claimed that greater economies could be achieved by using shorter sea corridors and that many users of the ferry would prefer a route which involved less time at sea. B & I Line vessels had also experienced tidal difficulties whilst using Swansea. The *Connacht* made the first-ever trip from Cork to Pembroke Dock on 21st May 1979 and Swansea disappeared pro tem from the list of car ferry ports.

When B & I Line closed the Swansea service it did result in economies of operation. However in the Swansea years many foot passengers used the service. They found that the very good train service from Swansea to London Paddington was ideal for onward travel.

Pembroke Dock proved a very different proposition as the town was situated on the end of a branch line which was single tracked and burdened with unmanned level crossings. These required the train's guard to get down from the diesel rail-cars serving the line and open and close the gates. Rail journeys now took two hours longer than before and the passengers deserted to the airlines. Car drivers too were not over-pleased with the poor roads in the Pembroke area.

The *Connacht* was in every way a successful ferry; indeed so successful that Verolme received an order for a sister ship *Leinster*. It had been noted that *Connacht's* dimensions were such that she could berth in the Waterloo Docks at Liverpool through the Waterloo Lock. The *Leinster*, it was announced would operate from Dublin to Liverpool. She was launched on 7th November 1980 by Mrs. Kathleen Reynolds, whose husband Albert later became Taoiseach (Prime Minister) of Ireland.

Following the *Connacht's* introduction to the Cork-Swansea-Pembroke routes, B & I Line transferred the *Innisfallen* to run with her sister *Leinster* and half sister *Munster* between Dublin and Liverpool. A three-ship service commenced but a very big fall-off occurred in traffic to Ireland because of civil unrest in Northern Ireland. In 1980 the *Innisfallen* was sold to Corsica Ferries and was renamed *Corsica Viva*. She has since seen much service in the Mediterranean Sea and in 1994 was operating as the *Caribia Viva* from Guadaloupe. In early 1995, renamed *Spirit of Independence*, she briefly operated between Folkestone and Boulogne for Meridian Ferries, a freight ferry company.

B & I Line went to Italy for a temporary replacement vessel in 1980 and on 13th February that year, the Sardinian registered *Espresso Olbia* arrived in Cork to cover for the *Connacht* which had gone to service the Liverpool route during dry docking and overhaul of that route's vessels. This ship had operated in earlier times on Britain's east coast as the *Tor Anglia* between Immingham – Gothenburg. With a gross tonnage of 7,300 she proved popular and retained her Italian officers, engineers and deckhands whilst B & I Line provided pursers and catering staff.

In September 1980 the *Connacht* transferred permanently to Dublin to be replaced by the 1969 built *Leinster*. No amount of rationalising could disguise the fact that a much smaller and

The *Expresso Olbia* (ex *Tor Anglia*) relieved the *Connacht* during 1980 whilst the Cork-based vessel was sent to Liverpool to cover overhauls on the Dublin service. *(Jack Phelan)*

older ferry had replaced the ferry of the future and when B & I renamed this ship *Innisfallen* it was clear that as far as Cork was concerned, the *Connacht* would not be back.

At this stage it should be mentioned that B & I Line were now making it clear that they were dissatisfied with the long passage up the River Lee to Cork City. They claimed that economies could be achieved and also better turn around time if a terminal nearer the harbour mouth was provided and in due course a dredging and land in-fill scheme at Ringaskiddy was started and plans for a new deep water port and ferry terminal were announced. Ringaskiddy was duly built and opened but up to the 2nd February 1983, B & I continued to use Tivoli.

Continuing civil unrest in Northern Ireland, oil crises and galloping inflation in Britain and Ireland had dealt savage blows to tourism and soon the B & I Line were talking of rationalisation. This meant that Rosslare-Pembroke and Cork-Pembroke would in future be operated by one vessel, the renamed *Innisfallen*. She did her best, sailing from Cork to Pembroke, a quick departure to Rosslare, back again to Pembroke, and then to Cork and so on. Time-keeping in bad weather with a ship 5 knots slower than her earlier car ferry namesake *Innisfallen* meant that sailings occasionally were cancelled, and these were usually Cork sailings!

The end was nigh and on 2nd February 1983 B & I closed their sailings to Cork. A service which traced its beginnings to 1822 was ended – but in the immortal words of St. Augustine *Not yet*. Having been given a special grant from the Irish Government, B & I chartered the splendidly appointed *Fennia* of 6,397 tons, carrying 1,200 passengers and 225 cars from Silja Line and commenced to run from Ringaskiddy to Pembroke Dock. The *Fennia*, with an Irish crew and an extra Finnish Captain, operated from 16th June to 28th September 1983. The *Fennia* did not have stabilisers; it had a swimming pool, an amenity which often could not be utilised because of the lack of stabilisers. The days grow short when they reach September so says the song – and so it was for Cork. B & I ended its passenger connection with Cork finally with the *Fennia's* last

The Silja Line vessel *Fennia* was chartered by B & I in a final attempt to make the Cork-Pembroke Dock service work as a viable proposition. She is seen here arriving at the Pembrokeshire port. *(Miles Cowsill)*

sailing. B & I Line sold the fifth *Innisfallen* to Strintzis Line in November 1986 following service from Rosslare to Fishguard and also to Pembroke Dock; she then took service between Ancona (Italy) & Patras (Greece) as the *Ionian Sun*. The Company claimed at the time that the revived summer service had run at a very big loss and that economies dictated that they concentrate on short sea routes only. And this is exactly what they eventually did, closing the Dublin to Liverpool route and reopening a direct Dublin Port to Holyhead service instead.

SEASPEED FERRIES

Seaspeed Ferries operated a ferry service in the seventies between Dublin and Barry in South Wales. Following negotiations with Cork Harbour Commissioners, the Company decided to operate between Barry and Cork and their ro-ro ferry *Seaspeed Ferry* duly arrived in Cork on the inaugural run on 14th January 1974.

At that time Fords had an assembly plant and their Irish Headquarters in Cork and in addition to assembling certain types of vehicles in the city they imported large numbers of ready to run vehicles. Seaspeed secured this contract.

The service was very successful and grew from once weekly to twice weekly. On 29th October 1974 their ferry *Seaspeed Challenger* came to Tivoli Ferryport for the first time.

Seaspeed complained of a lack of co-operation from the B & I Line in the use of the linkspan; whilst using Cork they continued to serve Dublin and in the latter part of 1975 a decision was made to concentrate their efforts on the Dublin-Barry route. This decision was partly due to the ending of a charter to them of the *Ulster Sportsman* and its return to its owners and Seaspeed Ferries terminated its Barry to Cork link in October 1975. The *Ulster Sportsman* at a later date was chartered to Truckline for its service from Poole and took the name *Dorset*.

Seaspeed Ferries established a ferry service between Dublin and Barry in 1974. Their chartered vessel *Seaspeed Challenger* is seen here leaving Cork. *(Cork Harbour Commissioners)*

WELSH IRISH FERRIES LIMITED 1983

In 1983 a consortium established a new freight ro-ro service between Barry and Cork (Ringaskiddy). This was to fill the vacuum created by B & I Line deciding to withdraw from ferry operations on the Cork-Pembroke Service.

The service commenced on 1st April, 1983 and was greeted with enthusiasm in both countries; the consortium chartered the *Ugland Trailer*, a typical ro-ro freighter of its time, but the Norwegian ship served only for a few months.

The service was not financially viable and closed suddenly without prior notice. The last sailing was on 1st July 1983.

In 1983 a consortium established a new freight ferry service between Barry and Cork, using the newly established terminal at Ringaskiddy. The *Ugland Trailer*, which was chartered by the Company, is seen here unloading at the Irish port. *(Finbarr O'Connell Photography)*

BRITTANY FERRIES 1978 TO DATE

Passenger trade from Cork to France had flourished for very many years. Trans-Atlantic liners both east and west bound, traditionally called at Cobh (formerly Queenstown) and it used to be possible to take passage on east bound ships to Cherbourg, Le Havre, Rotterdam, Bremen and Hamburg. Great liners such as Cunards' two Queens, US Lines' *United States* and *America* and many ships of Dutch, German and Greek liner companies also used Cobh. The Jumbo Jet killed that traffic, and today the *QE 2* calls once or twice a year, either as a cruise ship or on positioning trips to the United States. Cobh now has a cruise vessel terminal and cruise ships make many calls but these do not form part of the ferry scene.

Early in 1978 Brittany Ferries announced that they were commencing a service from the Breton port of Roscoff to Cork. Their ship would be their flagship the *Armorique*, which measured

Brittany Ferries' graceful *Armorique* is seen here turning off the Tivoli ferry port in Cork City following her arrival from Roscoff. *(Jack Phelan)*

5,372 gross tons. The ship would come to Cork from Roscoff on Friday nights arriving around mid-day and departing from Cork at 15.00 hours on Saturdays to give an early morning arrival in Roscoff on Sunday mornings. Brittany Ferries announced that the *Armorique* would run between Plymouth and Santander in Spain twice weekly with a service from Plymouth to Roscoff to position the vessel for the Cork run.

A special trip was made to Cork by the *Armorique* arriving on the morning of 17th March 1978, St. Patrick's Day. She docked at the South Custom Quay, within sight and sound of the City Hall. Breton groups travelled over and marched in Cork's Annual St. Patrick's Day Parade. Large numbers of Corkonians visited this novel arrival and marvelled at how French and different she was. The ship could accommodate 700 passengers and 160 cars. She had been built in 1972 at Le Havre as the *Terje Vigen* and Brittany Ferries purchased her in 1975.

Prior to the start of regular service, another Brittany ship *Penn ar Bed* arrived on a special trip, again at the South Custom House Quay. This was on 4th May 1978. The *Penn ar Bed* (2,891 gross tons) could accommodate 50 freight vehicles and 250 passengers. It was possible to vary the mix of vehicles between cars and freight. The regular weekly service commenced on 27th May 1978.

The *Armorique* used Tivoli Ferryport in her first year while end of season sailings were taken by the smaller *Penn ar Bed*. The service was most successful, the only adverse comments being the lack of stabilisers and the absence of proper restaurant facilities and it was no surprise when Brittany Ferries announced that carryings in 1979 were so encouraging that the chartered freighter *Normandia* would come to Cork at weekends during summer season to carry truck and trailer traffic and leave the vehicle decks on the *Armorique* free for holidaying motorists.

A surprise visitor to Cork on 3rd March 1979 was the *Prince of Brittany* (5,475 gross tons). This ship could carry 1,060 passengers and 220 cars. The regular vessel was unable to come and

The *Cornouailles* pictured at Ringaskiddy ferry port whilst covering on the Roscoff-Cork service. *(Jack Phelan)*

the "Prince" was sent to cover. It was her first visit; her next would be in very different circumstances. The *Prince of Brittany* was a sister ship to Irish Continental Line's *Saint Patrick* and had been built in 1970 as the *Prince of Fundy*.

On 31st March 1979 the *Cornouailles* arrived at Tivoli from Roscoff. The *Cornouailles* was built in 1977 and was of 3,382 tons and her capacity was 500 passengers and 240 cars. In fact the *Cornouailles* replaced the *Penn ar Bed* for the autumn sailings to Cork as bookings were heavier than expected. The *Normandia* was unable to come to Cork on one of her sailings in July 1979 and so the hastily chartered *RO/RO Dana* arrived at Tivoli from Roscoff on Sunday 1st July 1979.

The 1980 season was opened by the *Cornouailles* while the *Armorique* had charge of the high season sailings. It speaks volumes for the vision of Brittany Ferries that in the space of three seasons their ship had now become too small in summer to handle the volume of freight and private cars and so it was necessary again to put on a freight ship at peak periods. The *Breizh Izel* (2,768 gross tons) was now a weekly visitor to Tivoli and on certain Saturdays ferry lovers could capture the *Armorique* and the *Breizh Izel* executing intricate movements in Cork. In 1978 those in the know predicted that a Cork-Roscoff service could not be made viable, and within two years two vessels were in regular use at weekends. The *Breizh Izel* had been built in 1970 as the *Iniochos Express* and when Brittany Ferries sold her in 1989, she was converted to a passenger and car ferry and renamed *Duchess M.*.

The *Penn ar Bed* was the ship which Brittany Ferries used to commence the 1981 time-table. The trusted *Armorique* continued to operate between Cork and Roscoff while bookings for cars, freight and passengers built steadily.

Brittany Ferries had announced that in 1981 their newly chartered *Tregor* would be starting a new service to Dun Laoghaire. As is well known the *Tregor* never materialised – and Dun Laoghaire still has no Breton connection. The *Breizh Izel* did not come in 1981, but ran instead to Rosslare on an integrated Irish Continental/Brittany Ferries freight service. The chartered Portsmouth -St. Malo ferry *Goelo* made her one and only visit on 15th March 1981. The *Goelo* had a gross tonnage of 5,149, and ran for two years between Britain and France.

Big changes occurred in 1982. The Breton company chartered the ferry *Nils Dacke*, renamed her *Quiberon* and put her on the services to Santander and to Cork. The ship's gross tonnage was 7,950, her speed was much superior to that of the *Armorique* and she had an increased capacity for vehicles and passengers. Now Brittany Ferries could accommodate 1,140 passengers and could carry 286 cars.

The *Quiberon* never served Tivoli. Brittany Ferries were quite satisfied to use Cork Harbour Commissioners' new ferry port at Ringaskiddy and since 1982 the harbour terminal has been used by all the ferry companies trading to Cork. This ship established new standards on ferries to Ireland. Twelve years later she is still a popular vessel on early and late season sailings between Brittany and Ireland.

In October 1982 the *Prince of Brittany* arrived back at Cork. She was cruising from Normandy and berthed at the North Custom House Quay. She departed with her cruising clientele to Swansea, thus reviving memories of B & I Line's abandoned service. Brittany Ferries subsequently renamed the ship *Reine Mathilde* for service between Portsmouth and Caen and she became the *Beauport* in a fourth reincarnation on the Poole to Channel Islands service of British Channel Island Ferries.

1983 was a year of consolidation; little change and the *Quiberon* worked the route as usual. In 1984 the *Benodet* (4,371 gross tons) made her first call arriving at and departing from Ringaskiddy on 5th May. However, the *Quiberon* still ran to Santander and Plymouth during the week and on Friday nights left Roscoff for Cork, returning as usual on Saturday afternoons for the convenient early morning arrival on Sundays in Roscoff.

An old favourite returned to Cork Harbour on 23rd March 1985. The pioneering ferry *Armorique* was at Ringaskiddy and in the autumn Brittany Ferries sent their *Tregastel* to Cork.

A fire on board the *Quiberon* marred the early part of the 1986 season. Although it did little damage, a French tourist died and, following repairs, the *Quiberon* continued as before. In 1987 a new company, Swansea Cork Ferries, had revived the ferry service between the two cities. Brittany Ferries helped enormously in the setting up of the new company including organising and setting up of booking and office procedures. Brittany Ferries decided that they needed extra space and they came to a chartering arrangement with Swansea Cork.

As a result the Polish flagged, *Celtic Pride* commenced mid-week sailings for Brittany Ferries. The additional services were during the high season, so the *Quiberon* and the *Celtic Pride* worked in tandem. It is believed that Roscoff had never before been served by a ferry with a non-French Crew. The *Celtic Pride* had been built in France in 1972 for service in Finland. She was then called *Aalottar* and was of 7,801 gross tons. Acquired by Polferries she was renamed *Rogalin* and renamed again when chartered by Swansea Cork Ferries. In 1983 she had been chartered to Farskip as the *Edda*.

An old friend in new colours had arrived in Ringaskiddy on 23rd March 1987. It was the *Cornouailles* bedecked in the hull and funnel colours of Truckline, the Brittany Ferries freight

This fine view shows the **Quiberon** approachingRingaskiddy ferry port with Cobh in the background. *(Jack Phelan)*

division. As it came into Cork it crossed the French car carrier *Hunaudieres* coming down river from the former ferry terminal at Tivoli where it had delivered a consignment of trade cars. The *Cornouailles* shared Ringaskiddy that week-end with the *Mercandian Ocean*, a Ro/Ro vessel taking out articulated trucks loaded with meat.

1988 season had the *Quiberon* at week-ends and *Celtic Pride* mid-week operating in the high season. Carryings were good and there was talk of a bigger ship in the offing. This ship was the *Bretagne*. It was hoped that it would be ready for the start of the high season in 1989, but delays in fitting-out meant that once again Cork was host to the *Quiberon*. There were no mid-week sailings in 1989 as the *Celtic Pride* had returned to her original name of *Rogalin* and Poland, and so week-end sailings only were the order of the day.

The *Bretagne* finally arrived and took over in the latter half of July 1989; Brittany Ferries had commenced their service to Cork in 1978 with the 5,732 gross tons. *Armorique* – "too big" said the critics. Now eleven years later the 8,314 gross tons. *Quiberon* ["much too big" said the same critics] was replaced by the 23,000 gross tons *Bretagne*, carrying 2,030 passengers and 580 cars. The *Bretagne* had 580 cabins and now serves the route from St. Malo to Portsmouth. It also sees service in the winter between Portsmouth and Santander in Spain. The *Bretagne* rekindled memories of the vanished liners which once frequented Cobh.

1991 meant further changes on the Cork-Roscoff route. 1990 had been a year which had seen *Quiberon* operating in the shoulder periods with the *Bretagne* consolidating its position as the largest and finest ferry ever seen in Ireland. But at the season's commencement in 1991 Swansea Cork's *Celtic Pride* commenced running at week-ends for Brittany Ferries.

This was something completely new. The familiar slot now the preserve of an Irish operated, Polish owned ship. Indeed in a very short time the mixed Polish/Irish crew were firm favourites ashore in Roscoff and then came the *Bretagne* for her third summer season. September saw the *Celtic Pride* return to Roscoff again at weekends. The sea qualities of this ship were proved at this time when she was only one hour late arriving back at Cork after a voyage in rough seas when another ferry had taken nearly thirty hours to cross the same week-end from Fishguard to Rosslare.

Brittany Ferries felt that the increase in traffic in 1991 meant that they should operate all Cork-Roscoff services themselves, either with their own ships or ferries belonging to their affiliated or associated companies. And this is what they did in 1992. One of Brittany Ferries stalwarts returned on 14th March 1992 carrying its third name and the livery and hull colours of a third company, for Cork.

Unfortunately it was not a happy return for the *Cornouailles*– sailing as the *Havelet* of British Channel Island Ferries under charter to Brittany Ferries. Following a late arrival in Cork, her return journey to Roscoff was prematurely terminated when a freak wave struck the 3,382 gross ton ferry and caused serious listing and damage to the vehicles on the vehicle deck. She put back to Cork for emergency repairs, and left again on Monday 16th March, causing a furious row with the Irish Department of the Marine who claimed that they were not aware that she was departing and that their enquiries were not complete at the time of sailing. This was disputed by the ferry company.

The next arrival of the 1992 season at Cork saw a very different ferry on its first and only visit. This was the *Duc de Normandie*, 9,355 gross tons, an infinitely better vessel for the long sea crossing. The *Duc de Normandie* was built in 1978 as the *Prinses Beatrix* and ran between Harwich and the Hook of Holland under that name. The *Quiberon* then took over and *Bretagne* arrived back for a very successful high season.

Where will it all end? was the question posed in 1989. When Brittany Ferries announced a threefold increase in sailings to Ireland in 1993 at last even the critics were silenced. The plans called for an extra return sailing to Cork from Roscoff each week and a new service from Cork to St. Malo.

The *Quiberon* made the first arrival for Brittany at Cork on 3rd April 1993. Then came the *Val de Loire* which made its maiden Roscoff/Cork voyage, arriving on 12th June 1993. This ship measured 31,395 gross tons and then was, and currently still is, the largest ferry to come to Ireland. Most passengers agree that this ship is much more a cruise liner than a car ferry.

The statistics are impressive. Passenger capacity is 2,140, 543 cabins provide 1,686 berths and 600 cars can be accommodated. Superb restaurants and other passenger facilities make the voyage an unforgettable

In 1992, the **Duc de Normandie** made a one and only visit to Cork Harbour whilst covering on the Roscoff service. The vessel is seen here unloading at the Irish port. *(Jack Phelan)*

LET'S DRIVE DIRECT TO HOLIDAY FRANCE

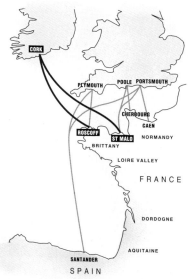

With us, your holiday starts the moment you step on board and at such good value too.

Choose from two direct routes;
Cork to Roscoff
Cork to St Malo

Enjoy luxurious cruise-ferries, convenient sailings and drive off in civilised ports far closer to all the finest holiday regions of Holiday France.

So head directly for our brochures and discover the best choice of holidays.

An afternoon scene at Cork in June 1990, with the *Bretagne* leaving for Roscoff. *(Miles Cowsill)*

experience and a swimming pool enables the energetic to get in water practice.

On the 20th June 1993, Brittany Ferries used the *Duchesse Anne* to start a second service linking Roscoff and Cork and also to commence a Cork-St. Malo link.

The *Duchesse Anne* had been purchased from the B & I Line during 1988; she was of course the Cork built *Connacht*, inaugurator of the Cork-Pembroke Dock service in 1979. The *Duchesse Anne* had been drastically altered internally at least twice since her launching although Brittany Ferries have reinstated much of the cabin space which had earlier been removed by the B & I Line.

The *Duchesse Anne's* initial arrival was slightly delayed by the late departure of a ferry occupying the berth at Ringaskiddy. The Breton company marked the return of the former Cork favourite by hosting a reception to which they invited Capt. Seamus Sydenham, her former Master of many years, and Mr. Patrick Martin who had been her designer at Verolme.

The *Duchesse Anne* then inaugurated the Cork-St. Malo service on Monday 21st June, and sailed back from St. Malo the following day, returning to Roscoff from Cork on 23rd June. Following a hugely successful season, the *Quiberon* took the end of season sailings.

1994 was a repeat of 1993. The *Quiberon* opened and closed the season. The *Val de Loire* ran to Cork on Friday nights, and the *Duchesse Anne* operated the second Roscoff service and consolidated the extremely successful St. Malo to Cork service for an extended period. Cork to Roscoff was and is the shortest direct route between Ireland and mainland Europe.

BRITTANY FERRIES TO IRELAND - THE FRENCH CONNECTION

Ian A. Carruthers

It was in 1978 that Brittany Ferries began their first route between France and Ireland, operating a mix of freight and tourism traffic between Roscoff in Brittany and Cork. Since then, the route has grown to become one of the fastest growing and most popular of all Brittany Ferries' routes - particularly for French tourists holidaying in Ireland.

The introduction of the Cork-Roscoff route complemented Brittany Ferries' existing network, with the route beginning at the same time as the service between Plymouth and Santander in northern Spain. The same ship could sail from Cork to Roscoff, then on to Plymouth and Santander, before returning to Cork via Roscoff again.

The Irish service really took off when Brittany Ferries launched the first of their superferries, the "Bretagne" in 1989, and added the Cork to St Malo route in 1993. Since then, numbers of passengers on the route have increased enormously. By 1994, total passengers numbered over 121,000 sailing from Cork to Roscoff and St Malo three times a week. This represents an impressive 31% of the direct ferry passenger market between Ireland and the continent.

A major benefit to the local economy comes from bringing French tourists to Ireland. The French tourist is one of the hardest to attract to holiday overseas; they tend to prefer the Riviera or the beaches of western France to the uncertain climate of the British Isles. However, Ireland holds a special magic for the French. A long history of co-operation and communication that goes back centuries means that Ireland holds a special place in the affections of the French, and vice versa.

Today, Brittany Ferries offers the French visitor to Ireland cottages, hotels, and the one thing that cannot be found in France - "Le Bed and Breakfast"! More and more French tourists are booking their entire holidays - travel and accommodation - through Brittany Ferries, and Ireland is high on their tourist shopping list.

With the numbers of passengers using Brittany Ferries service to and from Cork still growing, the French connection with Ireland is set to go from strength to strength!

Ian A. Carruthers
Managing Director (UK & Ireland)

IRISH CONTINENTAL AND IRISH FERRIES 1983 TO DATE

Prior to running their own service to Cork, Irish Continental Line had been involved with Brittany Ferries in the original plan to connect Cork with Continental Europe. Indeed the Irish Company were not pleased when the Breton Company announced the commencement of their service to Roscoff in 1978 and initiated High Court proceedings for an injunction to restrain Brittany Ferries from inaugurating the service. Thankfully the legal case did not go ahead and Brittany Ferries became the first operator from Cork to Europe.

Irish Continental Line had a complicated history, but in effect was a subsidiary of Irish Shipping Limited, a State-owned company set up in the 1939-45 war to provide a deep sea Merchant Navy for an Ireland which found itself bereft of shipping. The ferry company was so successful that, when in the course of time Irish Shipping Limited was liquidated, the Irish Continental Line survived its parent's demise.

In 1983 the ferry company commenced to run from Cork to Le Havre. The *Cork Examiner* on Friday, 7th January 1983 carried a news item reporting that the service would commence from Le Havre on Thursday 23rd June and that the first sailing from Cork would leave the following day. It also reported that the last sailing of the season would be outward bound from Cork on 2nd September.

Rosslare interests were outraged by Irish Continental's move; the County Wexford port had enjoyed a monopoly of ship calls from Le Havre and Cherbourg and much pressure was applied to the Irish Company not to share their traffic with Cork. Irish Continental were not moved from their decision and Ringaskiddy now played host to the *Saint Killian II* and *Saint Patrick II*. The service ran as scheduled in 1983.

The *Saint Killian II* was built for Stena Line AB in 1973 as the *Stena Scandinavica*. She was purchased by Irish Continental Line in 1978 and renamed *Saint Killian*. The Company had her stretched in Holland in 1981 and her gross tonnage became 10,256 with space for 2,000 passengers and 280 cars.

Both ferries continued to operate to France from Rosslare and each ship came to Ringaskiddy every other week-end. Following her stretching, the *Saint. Killian II* was Ireland's largest ferry and at that time was the largest ferry to operate from Cork Harbour.

The *Saint Patrick II* was also built in 1973. Originally the *Aurella*, (7,984 gross tons) she carries 300 cars and 1,630 passengers. The Irish company purchased and renamed her in 1982.

The initial season was extremely successful and Irish Continental continued to serve Le Havre and Cork with their two ferries. The passage was scheduled for 21.5 hours, but the length of the journey has never caused a booking shortage. By operating in the high season only, the loss which would be suffered in a twelve month schedule has been avoided.

With such success it was only a matter of time before the question of a service to Cherbourg would arise. In fact such a service did commence, and once again by clever scheduling, the *Saint Killian II* and the *Saint Patrick II* have been able to work the routes

Irish Ferries' *Saint Patrick II* seen discharging at Ringaskiddy ferry port. This view shows the vessel in the company's new livery established in 1995. *(Jack Phelan)*

from Rosslare to Cherbourg, Rosslare to Le Havre, Cork to Cherbourg and Cork to Le Havre.

Following a decision to become a Public Limited Company (PLC), the four routes are now marketed as Irish Ferries, controlled by Irish Continental Group PLC. The owning Company achieved a notable coup when early in 1994 it purchased the *Pride of Bilbao*. The *Pride of Bilbao* measures 37,583 gross tons, was built in 1986 and her passenger capacity is 2,500. She carries 600 cars and started her career as the *Olympia*, operating on the Viking Line service between Sweden and Finland. This huge ferry was and still is under charter to P. & O. European Ferries, but speculation has been rife as to what use the vessel will be put to when, or if, it becomes available to Irish Ferries.

In 1991 the Irish Continental Group eventually purchased B & I Line from the Irish Government and since January 1995 all their Irish Sea and European services have been operated and marketed as Irish Ferries. A plan to open new routes to Brest in the summer of 1995 was cancelled because of opposition from French Government sources. However, Irish Ferries have always been resourceful and having being foiled, temporarily at least, in their ambition to serve Brest decided to commence new services from Ireland to Roscoff.

Having only two ferries available to serve Rosslare, Cork, Le Havre, Cherbourg and Roscoff requires very clever and slick schedules. In 1995 Rosslare was connected to Roscoff in May, June and early July, but the Cork-Roscoff route runs once weekly on Fridays from

2nd June to 15th September from Roscoff. Cork departures were timetabled for 17.00 hours arriving next day at 10.00 hours, whilst the Irish Ferries vessels depart from Roscoff at 17.30 hours arriving in Cork at 10.30 on Sunday mornings. Sad to say the proposed new services to Roscoff did not find an enthusiastic welcome from the authorities controlling Roscoff and it was only following intervention by the European Commissioner for Transport that Irish Ferries were able to start up their Breton connection.

1995 promised to bring a highly competitive edge to ferry services serving Brittany. It is perhaps the full turn of the circle as at long last the original intention of services involving Brittany Ferries and the Irish Continental Group first mentioned in 1977, has become a reality.

SWANSEA CORK FERRIES 1987 TO DATE

Cork's Welsh connection died in 1983. Tivoli had been abandoned as a passenger ferry terminal the previous year, and whilst few regretted the severing of the connection to Pembroke Dock, the cessation of ferry services to Wales provoked a demand for someone – anyone to reinstate a ferry from Cork to Swansea. Cork Harbour Commissioners contacted British Transport Docks Board at Swansea and a joint report "The Emerald Gateway" was commissioned. Existing ferry operators however favoured the short sea philosophy and were reluctant to provide what they saw as a long sea service. Cork Harbour Commissioners persisted in their efforts to get a service going.

Swansea-Cork Ferries *Celtic Pride* seen at Cork City dressed overall during her first season. (*Jack Phelan*)

The *Cork Examiner* of 19th January 1984 carried the exciting news that Irish Transport Minister Jim Mitchell, had given approval to Irish Continental Line to become involved in a new ferry link between Cork and Swansea.

The very next morning the *Cork Examiner* had a very different story as its front page head-liner. Mr. Aubrey McElhatton of Irish Continental described the previous day's Ministerial announcement as "unfortunate and premature". In fact Mr. McElhatton said that they had not even discussed it at board level. Irish Continental did not become involved.

In 1987 three local authorities in Ireland, Cork Corporation, Cork County Council and Kerry County Council, together with West Glamorgan County Council and Swansea City Council co-operated to form a new company Swansea Cork Car Ferries Limited, and the *Celtic Pride* arrived at Ringaskiddy on 13th April 1987.

"This" said Mr. James McMahon, the new Company's first Managing Director, "is the finest ferry available anywhere". Facilities would include a swimming pool, sauna, casino, a chamber orchestra, hairdressing salon, children's playroom, a nursery as well as restaurants, duty free facilities, bars and the services of a resident doctor and nurse would be available on the ferry.

Indeed they were available, disappointingly the chamber orchestra turned out to be two Polish dance bands – but in 1987 no one used to British-Irish ferry travels ever expected facilities like swimming pools or hair dressing saloons. The ship had previously been in service from Poland to Sweden as the *Rogalin* and had when introduced to the Celtic Sea a Polish crew with Irish supervisory staff including On-Board Manager (Purser), Duty Free Managers, Master at Arms, and Hostess/Receptionist.

Initially there were language difficulties, as was only to be expected. The service proved exceptionally popular with the people of South Wales and Cork and Kerry but one shortcoming proved hard to overcome. The ferry had quite small and restricted vehicle decks and had a nominal capacity of 170 cars. With two car decks in full use freight could only be carried in minuscule quantities.

Because of excellent relations with Brittany Ferries the *Celtic Pride* operated a mid-week return service to Roscoff for Brittany in addition to its South Wales sailings. The ferry proved popular with French motorists and passengers. The coming of Swansea Cork Ferries provoked a savage price cutting war with the two established operators Sealink and B & I Line and accusations of Government subsidies and unfair advantages through using a non EEC crew. There was also resentment over the fact that not many British or Irish nationals were being employed on the ferry; critics tended to gloss over the number of Welsh and Irish shore staff employed in offices on both sides of the sea and the employment of local dockers and the regional tourism benefits in both Wales and Ireland.

1988 was a repeat of the first season; again the *Celtic Pride* sailed to Swansea and Roscoff. The popular vessel had set standards of facilities on board, which meant that other companies were now obliged to provide similar standards. However there had been management troubles; Chief Executives had come and gone and the Company were anxious to secure a vessel with a larger car deck for 1989.

A reflective view of the *Celtic Pride* arriving early at Ringaskiddy from Swansea. *(Jack Phelan)*

The Irish Government had originally been supportive of the venture, but despite talk and promises of promises, certain guarantees of funding were too slow in materialising and so 1989 proved a blank year. No ferry, no service and the critics were nodding wisely. "Told you so" was the chorus.

The Directors were most anxious to prove the critics wrong. Accordingly visits were arranged to Greece and a management structure which was to be unique evolved. From Cork County Council, Mr. Paddy Deasy, was seconded to the Company as Managing Director and Cork Corporation provided senior staff member Thomas Hunter McGowan as Financial Controller. The formidable John Power, for many years a Chief Purser with B & I Line, returned as Operations Manager and marketing was tackled and put on a sound footing.

May 1990 saw the blue hulled Greek owned ferry *Ionian Sun* arrive at Ringaskiddy. The vessel was never officially renamed but traded as the *Celtic Pride II*. It had a familiar shape – it was in fact the former B & I car ferry *Leinster* built in Cork in 1968, renamed *Innisfallen* (5) in 1980, sold to Strintzis Line in 1986 and was now back within sight of its birthplace, Rushbrooke.

Strintzis Lines had remodelled the ship's interior; she now boasted many more cabins above the car decks, she had a better vehicle capacity and could carry more freight. Unfortunately it was not possible for Brittany Ferries to operate her to Roscoff given the lateness of her charter arrangements and the *Ionian Sun* trading as the *Celtic Pride II*, only

Above: The Polish-registered *Celtic Pride* is seen here swinging at Kennedy Quay. *(Jack Phelan)*
Below: In 1990 Swansea Cork Ferries chartered the Greek-owned ferry *Ionian Sun* (ex *Leinster*) to run their ferry service. The vessel is seen here arriving at Swansea. *(Miles Cowsill)*

An early morning view of the Greek-registered *Superferry* manoevring to the layby berth with the Cork Pilots vessel in attendance. (*Jack Phelan*)

operated for the 1990 season for Swansea Cork Ferries. The very short season did not allow the Greek crew to acclimatise in the same way as the Polish crew on the original *Celtic Pride* and she failed to attain the popularity of her predecessor.

Carryings for 1990 were good; indeed both afloat and ashore the demand was for the Company to operate a longer season; some went further and demanded an all-year service. The passage from Cork to Swansea occupied ten hours; the daylight crossing from Cork proved popular with passengers who were inclined to look upon the trip as a cruise. Night crossings from Swansea gave the chance of quite a lengthy rest in bed or with a Pullman seat and arrival at a sensible hour in the morning. Many passengers appreciated not having to leave the ferry at 3 a.m.

The *Celtic Pride II* did not boast a chamber orchestra but it did have a magnificent grand piano situated in the forward lounge. When the ferry returned to Greece at the end of the season, it was announced that the original *Celtic Pride* was returning from Poland for 1991.

In the 'off season' a strange thing happened. During a press conference being given by Sealink in Dublin a virulent attack was made on Swansea Cork Ferries and its continued existence; The rival operation suggested that Government funds, if there were any available, would be better employed building a super highway from Cork to Rosslare – this would ensure that ferries operating from the Wexford port would be more easily available to Cork and Kerry people.

A spirited answer was given in the *Evening Echo* of Cork. "Why" asked that paper "is Goliath worried about David?". The sight of the world's leading ferry operator railing against a one ship operation did indeed justify the Goliath and David analogy. Indeed the 'Echo' reminded its readers that in a previous famous encounter Goliath had lost to David.

The *Celtic Pride* (ex *Rogalin*) was reintroduced to Cork-Swansea with some style. The directors of the Company held a pre-sailing reception on board the ferry in Ringaskiddy on Friday 1st March 1991, and a large party of VIPs dined on board the crossing and, following an early morning arrival in Swansea, the ferry, having discharged, moved in through the entrance locks and moored in the non-tidal docks. On Saturday night (2nd March) civic representatives from Swansea attended a special dinner and reception on board. Lord Mayors, Council Chairmen and Government Ministers all combined to make it a very special occasion.

And so the *Celtic Pride* settled down again sailing on the Inter-City route; but there was more to come as on Friday 15th March 1991 the Brittany Ferries route between Cork and Roscoff was reopened for the 1991 season; but it was not a French ship which restarted the route. The *Celtic Pride* was now to operate at week-ends for Brittany Ferries until May when they sent their own ferry back on service.

The 1991 season on the route between the Welsh and Irish centres proved to be a very good year. The *Celtic Pride* proved a popular vessel and bookings held steady. In the Autumn the *Celtic Pride* returned to the Roscoff-Cork run again at weekends and proved popular with Continental travellers.

Following the seasonal ending of the Breton route, several functions were held on Saturday nights on the *Celtic Pride* in Swansea. Bad weather struck on the very last trip of the season when she could not leave Ringaskiddy until 01.07 hours on 31st October and did not arrive in Swansea until 14.40 hours, instead of her scheduled 08.00 hours arrival. The crew and passengers had endured a very bad crossing indeed.

The 1992 season commenced on Friday 6th March 1992. Once again the *Celtic Pride* was the ship to run the service and one-week after its initial voyage she sailed up the River Lee to Cork City where she berthed at the North Custom House Quay. Here she was visited by Mr. Albert Reynolds T.D., the Irish Taoiseach. Many Dail members and local representatives were present and saw Mr. Reynolds unveil a plaque to mark his visit.

Competition on southern routes was intense all season. B & I Line had just introduced the *Isle of Innisfree* on their Pembroke Dock to Rosslare route, Stena Sealink were, as usual, operating the *Stena Felicity* so the Rosslare routes certainly held the edge as regards modern ships with very much larger capacity. Perhaps it was loyalty, perhaps stubbornness, but the *Celtic Pride* was still experiencing heavy bookings.

Tragedy struck in August 1992 when two teenagers, a brother and sister, died in their cabin en route to Cork. They had been overcome by fumes, traced to an alteration which had been made to the venting system in a septic tank. It proved impossible to determine where and when the alteration had been made.

As a result of the accident, certain sailings had to be cancelled and in an effort to catch up with reservations *Celtic Pride* sailed on at least two occasions to Pembroke Dock direct from Cork. As in 1991 a number of weekend functions were run on board the ship in Swansea. However there were no sailings to Roscoff by the *Celtic Pride* as Brittany Ferries had used their own tonnage all through the season. The last sailing of the year was made on Sunday night 1st November from Swansea to Cork. The *Celtic Pride* returned to her Polish owners and has since resumed her Polish name *Rogalin.*

In October 1992 the **Cork Examiner** carried the shock news that Swansea Cork Car Ferries Limited had been sold by its local authority owners to Strintzis Line of Greece. This was the company from whom *Ionian Sun*, trading as *Celtic Pride II*, had been chartered in 1990. The news of the sale was followed immediately by a further announcement that Swansea Cork Ferries would be chartering a Strintzis ferry for 1993.

So in 1993 another vessel arrived from Greece for the season. This was the Japanese built *Superferry*, which had been built in 1972 and originally was named the *Cassiopeia* for Ocean Ferry K.K. She became the *IZU No. 3* in 1976 and was acquired by the Greek company in 1991 and following a brief period as the *Ionian Star* became the *Superferry* She had been extensively rebuilt before coming to Cork. Her tonnage now is 7,454 gross tons, and the passenger capacity is 1,355 with space for 550 cars.

Prior to the *Superferry* coming to Ringaskiddy, Strintzis had spent a lot of money on putting in extra cabins, berths and Pullman seats and a new Irish Pub–Paddy Murphy's–had been installed.

The *Superferry* took up service on time in 1993. It had a much bigger capacity for

The **Superferry** seen at the linkspan pending her morning departure to Wales. *(Jack Phelan)*

vehicles, with two full width decks in contrast to its immediate predecessor. This extra capacity resulted in an immediate increase in freight carryings and the ship was given a longer season. She has proved a good sea-vessel and has extra speed to help in what is a very tight and demanding schedule.

The Company suffered two tragedies in 1993 with the sudden death of Chief Purser Bill Croft and the untimely passing of Operations Manager John Power. These two men had been ever-present since the revival of Swansea to Cork ferry services.

1993 and 1994 have seen ever-increasing numbers travelling between the south and south west coasts and regions of Ireland and Wales. The *Superferry* is not by any means the most elegant of ships; her lines are too squat but she does look and act like a ship, and not just a block of flats imposed on a garage. Again due to scheduling and weather problems, allied to a very occasional tidal problem the *Superferry* has on a few occasions in 1994 and 1995 sailed to Pembroke Dock. Denis Murphy continues to serve as Company Chairman, a position he has held since the formation of Swansea Cork Ferries.

SWANSEA CORK FERRIES - YOUNG AND SUCCESSFUL

Thomas Hunter McGowan

I am delighted to welcome the publication "Ferries of Cork" which charts the close links between ferry companies and the Port of Cork.

Shipping of all types has been a feature of Cork's life for centuries. The City's trade grew around its port and Cork's merchants have been trading internationally in a very significant way since the 17th century.

The ferries have evoked Cork's economic and social history over many generations. Sadly, for too many they will always be associated with involuntary emigration. These days, one is more likely to see ferry services used to carry holidaymakers and business people and, of course, freight conveying the products of industrial manufacture.

If the nature of ferry travel has changed over the years, there have also been radical changes in the size, appearance and comfort of passenger ferries.

For those used to the "functional" ferries - perhaps functional is too kind a term - plying between Cork and the UK over the years, Swansea Cork Ferries "The Superferry" must seem like luxury afloat. And indeed it is. The best-appointed and luxurious vessel to sail the southern corridor, The *Superferry* has a capacity for 1,400 passengers and 360 cars, excluding freight. It contains 444 berths, 296 Pullman seats, restaurants, shopping and leisure facilities.

The only service sailing directly from the UK to the South West Region, Swansea Cork Ferries represents a critical economic link whose importance cannot be over-emphasised. Its value to Cork and Kerry in particular can be gauged by the fact that it carries some 200,000 passengers annually, many being tourists who otherwise would access Ireland through the Eastern Seaboard and be lost to the Region.

The Swansea Cork Ferries story is a relatively young one. The service came into being following the withdrawal of B&I from Cork in the mid-1980s and since then ours is a significant success story.

We look forward to further growth in the years ahead.

Thomas Hunter McGowan

Thomas Hunter McGowan, Managing Director

This view shows Brittany Ferries' *Duchesse Anne* (ex *Connacht*) and Swansea Cork Ferries' *Superferry* at the layby berth at Ringaskiddy. *(Jack Phelan)*
The *Connacht* dressed overall in the heart of Cork City prior to her maiden sailing. *(Jack Phelan)*

CROSS RIVER FERRIES
(CARRIGALOE TO GLENBROOK)

For many years the difficulty of access from one side of Cork Harbour to the other presented an insurmountable problem for motorists with a trip of approximately twenty-six miles involved in getting from Cobh to Ringaskiddy if a vehicle was involved.

In 1993 Cork County Council and the newly formed Cross River Ferries Ltd., solved the problem. The Council provided ferry slips at Carrigaloe on Great Island, near Cobh and on the opposite side of the river at Glenbrook between Passage West and Monkstown.

Two former vehicle ferries *Kyleakin* and *Lochalsh* were purchased from Caledonian MacBrayne who operate ferries on Scotland's west coast and renamed *Carrigaloe* and *Glenbrook* respectively. These now operate an all day long service between the two locations and carry cars, mini-buses and trucks. There is also a big trade in foot passengers. Service commenced in March 1993. The *Carrigaloe's* gross tonnage is 225 and she is licensed to carry 200 passengers and 27 cars. The *Glenbrook* is of similar tonnage and capacity.

In the spring of 1995 it was announced that the service would be suspended for a period of five weeks. This was caused by the landing slips on each side of the river having been undermined and being declared unsafe. Immediate work was put in hand by Cork County Council and the service restarted in June, 1995. At the time of the temporary suspension 1,100 vehicles per day were being carried.

Marine Transport Services Ltd., one of the owners of the Cross River Company also operate passenger only ferries from Cobh to Haulbowline Island, whilst the Department of Defence run ferries for military and naval personnel from Cobh to Haulbowline and Spike Island. (See map page 8)

POSTCARDS & CORK FERRIES

Ferries and Passenger Ships of Cork have featured on post-cards at various times. There are postcards of all Brittany's passenger ferries which are trading to Cork presently or which came in the past. All of these with one exception show the Brittany vessels in French locations or at sea and as such are not relevant to Cork itself. The exception is a card issued in Ireland showing the *Duchesse Anne* leaving Cork.

Again, there are postcards showing the *Saint Killian II* and the *Saint Patrick II* at Rosslare. These, like Brittany Ferries postcards, do not show Cork locations or Cork services.

The two *Celtic Prides* have appeared on cards which do relate to Cork. The original *Celtic Pride* was shown on two cards which were sold on the ferry and depict the vessel as she was painted in 1988. At that time she carried, as always, a white hull with the name of the Company painted on the hull sides.

The *Superferry* of Swansea Cork Ferries is the subject of two cards. One shows the *Superferry* heading away from the camera and was used with a pre-printed offer of a bargain fare. The second card shows the vessel broadside on. A nice card is rather disfigured by the

Yes we do.

At AIB Bank we can provide all the expert advice and assistance you'll need when choosing a mortgage. Call in for your free homebuyers guide "A place of your own".

If you or a member of your family are buying a house in the future contact:

slogan "We've saved 400 miles".

The *Celtic Pride II* formerly *Leinster* and then the fifth *Innisfallen* was the subject of a postcard which was a sketch of the ship inward bound to Ringaskiddy with Cobh in the background. It was a black and white card. The artist was Philip Gray.

City of Cork and B & I vessels had many cards. The third *Innisfallen* can boast of at least eight different versions. The first was a painting of the ship showing her as first delivered with a dark green and cream hull, and the black topped, white banded, green funnel of B & I Steam Packet Company Limited. This appears to have been an official Company card.

The second card is photographic; indeed apart from the first card, all others are photographs. The second card shows the *Innisfallen* (3) berthed at Penrose Quay Cork. She is now in the livery and funnel colours of City of Cork S. P. Co. (1936) Ltd., and berthed just below her is one of the Irish Naval Service's three corvettes, an ex-Royal Navy Flower class ship. An elderly Italian steamer is berthed on South Quays next to the stern of one of Irish Shipping's Birkenhead-built turbine steamers.

The third and fourth cards show the *Innisfallen* (3) at Tivoli. Berthed astern is the *Glengariff* of the City of Cork S.P. Co. whilst the *Sanda* can just be made out astern of the *Glengariff* on one of these cards. Berthed at the South Quay is one of a fleet of cargo liners built after the war's end for Irish Shipping Limited.

The fifth postcard view of the *Innisfallen* (3) shows her at Penrose Quay with a motor vessel berthed at the South Quays. The latter appears to be Wexford Steam Ship Company's *Menapia*.

The sixth card shows the *Innisfallen* (3) in the early days of the B & I Line. The 'fertility sign' is on her funnel, the place is again Penrose Quay and a chartered German motor vessel the *Hans Knuppel* is under the Container crane which had been erected immediately down river of the passenger berth. The lift on-lift off service run by the German vessel replaced the conventional Liverpool ships.

The ship is viewed from North Custom House Quay in the seventh card. It differs from all other cards in that it shows a view of her stern and the photographer was positioned between the supports of the now-vanished heavy lift crane of Cork Harbour Commissioners.

The eighth card is a black and white view of Fishguard Harbour from Pencw. It shows the *Innisfallen* berthed at the Railway Station and in the left foreground the veteran steamer *St. Andrew* of Fishguard and Rosslare Railways and Harbours Board is arriving and about to berth.

The fourth *Innisfallen* (built in Germany in 1968) featured on at least four postcards. The first shows her as built passing Blackrock Castle Cork bound for Swansea. The B & I Line red "fertility" symbol is prominent on her funnel. The second post card shows the ferry still in original B & I finish and berthed at Tivoli. The next card is the first card, reissued, and now the *Innisfallen* (4) carries a stencilled B & I legend on her funnel. The card was a retouch job.

However the fourth card shows the *Innisfallen* arriving at Swansea. Again the vessel is in her original finish and judging from the shadow and reflection of the sun on water was taken between 6 and 7 p.m. as she came in to port following a daylight crossing from Cork.

The fifth *Innisfallen* started life as the *Leinster* and there are at least three postcards of her in that incarnation; all show her in Dublin Bay or at Dublin Ferryport. The two out in the bay show the legend B & I stencilled on the funnel while the third has the *Leinster* berthed in Dublin, at full tide and with the "fertility" sign on the funnel. She of course relieved in Cork as the *Leinster*.

When the *Leinster* became the fifth *Innisfallen* she featured on a postcard at Rosslare at a time when she was operating the triangular Cork – Pembroke Dock Rosslare service.

The *Connacht* was the subject of at least two postcards relating to her time in Cork; there was an excellent card available of her arriving in Pembroke Dock showing the newly erected high level road bridge there, when the *Connacht* was on the Cork - Pembroke Service. A second postcard shows her outward bound from Tivoli passing Cobh with St. Colman's Cathedral high on the hill above.

Since being sold to Brittany Ferries and renamed *Duchesse Anne* there have been at least two further cards of the ship. One shows her passing Whitepoint in Cork Harbour; the other was issued in France and shows a departure from St. Malo.

The post war *Munster* of B & I served for some months on the Cork to Fishguard route and although no trace of a postcard exists showing her whilst in Cork there is a beautifully taken card in full colour showing her berthed at a Mediterranean port as the *Orpheus*.

The *Guernsey Express* (ex *Viking IV* of Thoresen Car Ferries) is a regular visitor to the Port of Cork, The livestock vessel is seen here moored at Horgan's Quay. *(Jack Phelan)*

CORK FERRIES ELSEWHERE

Quite apart from ferries which served the Port of Cork, there are a number of vessels which were built in Cork Harbour for service elsewhere. The old dockyard at Rushbrooke had been put back into service during the emergency (1939 – 1945) to service the hastily assembled cargo fleet of Irish Shipping Ltd., and in the fifties this had taken on a new lease of life under Dutch owners and many bulk carriers were built by the newly-styled Verolme Cork Dockyard.

Verolme originally concentrated on bulkers, however when B & I Line decided to switch to car ferries as opposed to passenger only vessels, Verolme was entrusted with the building of their *Leinster*, which was a sister of the Rendsburg (Germany) built *Innisfallen* and a half-sister of the smaller *Munster*. The subsequent history of *Leinster* has been previously detailed in the sections dealing with Cork-Swansea and Cork-Pembroke Dock both with B & I Line and Swansea Cork Ferries.

The *Leinster* was a very successful vessel; it was no surprise that, when B & I Line decided to order a ro-ro freighter, they returned to Verolme. And so the *Dundalk* was built for them in 1974. The only time that the *Dundalk* ever returned to Cork Harbour was for overhaul at Verolme. Equally she never ran an Ireland-Britain service for B & I Line and was away on charters nearly all the time. When in 1983 Stena Line purchased her she ran as the *Stena Sailer* between Dun Laoghaire and Holyhead for Sealink and when Sealink took her over from Stena Line and renamed her *St. Cybi* she ran as a ro-ro ferry between Dun Laoghaire and Holyhead and between Rosslare and Fishguard.

B & I Line then ordered the 6,812 ton *Connacht* from Verolme. She was launched in 1978 and her career is dealt with in the section dealing with B & I Line's Cork-Swansea and Cork-Pembroke Dock. The *Connacht* was an outstanding success and sister *Leinster* was soon on the stocks at Verolme.

The *Leinster* was launched on 7th November 1980 but her delivery was delayed because of industrial unrest in the shipyard. Eventually following trials in Cork Harbour B & I Line took possession and she left Cork Harbour to serve her owners ever since, first on Dublin-Liverpool, then Dublin-Holyhead and since being renamed *Isle of Inishmore* on the Rosslare-Pembroke Dock and Dublin-Holyhead routes.

Verolme built two further car ferries, but of different designs and for very different services. The *Little Island Ferry* is a cable operated ferry running from Grantstown near Waterford City to Little Island in the middle of the River Suir. This small ferry was built at Rushbrook in 1968 and can carry six cars and their passengers. The service is used by guests crossing the King's Channel to Waterford Castle Hotel.

The *Strangford Ferry* was built by Verolme in 1969. It can carry 22 cars and 263 passengers and operates from Portaferry to Strangford at the mouth of Strangford Lough in County Down. There she operates in tandem with *Portaferry Ferry* which as the *Cleddau King* in earlier days ran between Pembroke Dock (Hobbs Point) and Neyland (formerly New Milford) and the original terminus for B & I Steam Packet Co. passenger ships from Cork.

Although not car ferries, Verolme built four Container vessels; two for B & I Line and two for British Rail/Sealink; the *Kilkenny* and the *Wicklow* were the ships built for B & I Line. They were built in 1973 and 1971; the *Kilkenny* was tragically sunk following collision with the German *Hasselwerder* in Dublin Bay. The *Wicklow* was sold by B & I Line in 1994. Both ships traded regularly for many years between Dublin, Cork and the Continent.

British Rail's container vessels were the *Rhodri Mawr* and the *Brian Boroime* which Verolme built in 1970. They were very similar vessels to the B & I Line ships and traded between Holyhead and Dublin and Holyhead and Belfast. They also came to Cork for a time in 1979 on a Holyhead-Cork specialised service. They have since been sold.

Verolme also built the Patrol vessels *Deirdre, Emer, Aisling* and *Aoife* and the helicopter carrier *Eithne* for the Irish Navy. All these ships are based at Haulbowline in Cork Harbour.

Prior to Verolme taking over at Rushbrooke and commencing ship-building there, the then Cork Dockyard Limited carried on a business of ship repairing and general dockyard work. In 1950 Cork Dockyard Limited were given the job of converting an ex-Royal Navy frigate to a car ferry. Thus emerged from Rushbrooke the *Halladale*, owned by Townsend Car Ferries and the vessel on which Townsend Car Ferries and later Townsend Thoresen built their fortunes.

In 1950, Cork Dockyard Ltd were given the job of converting an ex Royal Navy frigate for Townsend Car Ferries. The *Halladale* is seen here leaving Ireland for Dover after her conversion. *(Cork Examiner)*

FLEET LISTS

CITY OF CORK S.P. CO./B.&I.

CORK - FISHGUARD

NAME	YEARS ON ROUTE	TONNAGE	NOTES
Innisfallen (1)	1896 – 1918	1,400	War Casualty
Inniscarra	1903 – 1918		War Casualty
Kilkenny	1919		From B.&I. S.P.Co.
Glengariff (1)	1919		Disposed of 1924
Killarney (2)	1919 – 1920	1,500	Built as Moorfowl
Bandon	1920		Became Lady Louth
Maple	1920	1,300	Owned by Burns & Laird
Logic	1920 – 1921	900	Owned by Belfast S.S. Co.
Classic	1921 – 1924	1,500	Renamed Killarney 1924
Killarney	1924 – 1930	1,500	Takeover by Coast Lines
Innisfallen (2)	1930 – 1939	3,019	Sunk in W.W. II
Kenmare	1939 – 1948	1,700	Returned to Liverpool Service
Munster	1948	4,115	Now Orpheus
Innisfallen (3)	1948 – 1967	3,705	Sold to Greek Interests
Irish Coast	1952 – 1966	3,813	Relief Vessel

CORK - SWANSEA

NAME	YEARS ON ROUTE	TONNAGE	NOTES
Innisfallen (4)	1969 – 1979	4,848	Sold 1980 to Corsica
Lenister	1970 – 1979	4,899	Relief Vessel: became Innisfallen (5)
Stena Germanica	1978	5,195	Relief Vessel: lost as A.Regina
Connacht	1979	6,812	Sold in 1988: now Duchesse Anne

CORK - PEMBROKE DOCK

NAME	YEARS ON ROUTE	TONNAGE	NOTES
Connacht	1979 – 1980	6,812	Now Duchesse Anne
Espresso Olbia	1980	7,300	Relief Vessel: ex Tor Anglia
Leinster	1980	4,899	Renamed Innisfallen
Innisfallen (5)	1980 – 1983	4,899	Ex Leinster. Sold 1986
Fennia	1983	6,397	Charter from Silja Line

Above: B&I's cargo vessel *Wicklow* is seen here at Rushbrooke on one of her frequent visits to the port. *(Jack Phelan)*

Below: A typical early seventies scene in Cork Harbour with the B&I vessel *Innisfallen* outward bound to Swansea. *(Jack Phelan)*

CORK - LIVERPOOL

NAME	YEARS ON ROUTE	TONNAGE	NOTES
Innisfallen (1)	Early 20th Century	1,400	War Casualty
Kenmare	1921 – 1939	1,700	Transferred to Fishguard 1939-48
Innisfallen (2)	1939 – 1940	3,019	War Casualty
Bandon	1920 – 1931		Ex Louth
Ardmore (1)	1921 – 1930	1,700	Later Lairdshill
Ardmore (2)	1923 – 1940		WW II Casualty 12 Passengers only
Kenmare	1948 – 1956	1,700	Scrapped 1956
Glengariff	1956 – 1963	1,599	Ex Rathlin
Glanmire	1963 – 1968	789	Cattle & Cargo only

BRITTANY FERRIES

ROSCOFF/CORK - ST. MALO/CORK

NAME	YEARS ON ROUTE	TONNAGE	NOTES
Armorique	1978 – 1986	5,732	Ex Terje Vigen: Sold 1993 to China
Penn ar Bed	1978 – 1983	2,891	Sold in 1984: now Princess M
Cornuailles	1978 – 1987	3,382	Now Havelet/Condor Ferries
Prince of Brittany	1979 and 1982	5,465	Originally Prince of Fundy renamed Reine Matilde became Beauport One visit only each time
Normandia	1979	2,311	Freight vessel
Ro/Ro Dana	1979		Once only charter
Breizh Izel	1980	2,768	Freight only: Sold 1989: now Duchess M
Goelo	1981	5,149	Ex Viking 6 One visit only now Moby Dream,
Quiberon	1982 – 1994	8,441	Ex Nils Dacke
Benodet	1984	4,371	Ex Gelting Nord: became Corbiere
Tregastel	1985	3,999	Ex Njegos: became St. Clair
Celtic Pride	1987 – 1988	7,801	Charter from Swansea /Cork: now Rogalin
Bretagne	1989 – 1992	23,000	

NAME	YEARS ON ROUTE	TONNAGE	NOTES
Celtic Pride	1991	7,801	Charter from Swansea/Cork now *Rogalin*
Havelet	1992	3,382	Charter from BCIF: Once off
Duc de Normandie	1992	9,355	One visit only: ex *Prinses Beatrix*
Val de Loire	1993 to date	31,395	Ex *Nils Holgersson*
Duchesse Anne *	1993 to date	6,812	Ex *Connacht* (B & I)

* Operates on Roscoff-Cork and St. Malo-Cork Services.

CROSS RIVER FERRIES LIMITED

CARRIGALOE – GLENBROOK

Carrigaloe	1993 to date	225	Ex *Kyleakin*
Glenbrook	1993 to date	225	Ex *Lochalsh*

SWANSEA/CORK FERRIES

Celtic Pride *	1987 – 1988	7,801	Returned to Poland
Celtic Pride II †	1990	4,828	*Ionian Sun* Ex *Leinster*
Celtic Pride	1991 – 1992	7,801	Returned to Poland
Superferry ‡	1993 to date	7,454	Originally *Cassiopeia* then *Izu No. 3*

* Sailed on Roscoff Route 1987, 1988, 1991 – Sailed to Pembroke Dock twice in 1992.
† Named *Ionian Sun* but traded as *Celtic Pride II*
‡ Sailed to Pembroke Dock on diversions.

WELSH IRISH FERRIES LIMITED

CORK - BARRY

Ugland Trailer	1983	7,454	Returned to owner

CLYDE SHIPPING CO.

GLASGOW - DUBLIN - WATERFORD - CORK

Fastnet	1946 – 1950	1,415	Became *Greypoint*
Rathlin	1950 – 1952	1,599	Became *Glengariff*
Sanda	1952 – 1960	854	Cargo only

Above: Brittany Ferries' *Tregastel* is seen here at Cork on one of her visits to the port whilst covering on the Roscoff link. *(Jack Phelan)*
Below: An impressive view of the *Val de Loire* turning at Ringaskiddy ferry port outward bound for Roscoff. *(Miles Cowsill)*

Ferries of Cork

IRISH CONTINENTAL/IRISH FERRIES

CORK - Le HAVRE : CORK - CHERBOURG

NAME	YEARS ON ROUTE	TONNAGE	NOTES
Saint Killian II	1983 to date	10,256	Formerly *Stena Scandinavica* then *Saint Killian*
Saint Patrick II	1983 to date	7,984	Formerly *Aurella*

Both vessels operate Cork-Cherbourg and Cork-Le Havre and Cork-Roscoff routes.

SEASPEED FERRIES

CORK - BARRY

Seaspeed Ferry	1974 – 1975		
Seaspeed Challenger	1974 – 1975		
Seaspeed Trailer	1974 – 1975	1,279	Cypriot Registry
Ulster Sportsman	1975	1,000	Formerly *Donautal* later *Dorset, St. Magnus*

BIBLIOGRAPHY

I am indebted to all of the following publications from which much valuable information is available.

Irish Passenger Steam Ship Services Vols 1 & 2 — D.B. McNeill
Clyde & Other Coastal Steamers — Duckworth & Langmuir
Railway and Other Steamers — Duckworth & Langmuir
The B & I Line — Hazel P. Smyth
A History of the B & I Line and City of Cork S.P. Co. (1936) Ltd. — Ernest R. Reader
Clyde Shipping Co. Ltd. A History — Alan D. Cuthbert
Car Ferries of the British Isles — Nick Widdows
Ferries from Pembrokeshire — Miles Cowsill
Across the Irish Sea — Robert C. Sinclair
The Long Watch — Frank Forde
Brittany Ferries – From the Land to the Sea — Miles Cowsill
British Ferry Scene
Sea Breezes
Ships Monthly
Marine News (World Ship Society)
Cork Examiner and *Cork Evening Echo*

Above: The **Saint Patrick II** seen off Cobh in 1995 inward bound from Roscoff. *(Jack Phelan)*
Below: This early morning scene shows the **Superferry** arriving from Greece in March 1995 with the tug **Oyster Bank** in attendance. *(Jack Phelan)*

WHERE TO PHOTOGRAPH
SHIPS & FERRIES

With so many quays and docks in the Cork port area there are a number of good locations for the ship photographer. The quays in Cork City are all open and photographs can be taken of ships berthed and berthing. Since Cork is the head of navigation, all incoming ships have to swing either on arrival or immediately prior to departure and quite dramatic pictures can be taken of the really big ships being edged round by their attendant tugs.

The best photographic location for ships at Tivoli is the Marina Walk; this runs on the river bank opposite Tivoli from Blackrock pier up to the electricity generating station near the South Quays. Splendid views are available of ships coming up the Marina.

The river ferries can be photographed from the roads on either side of the river and naval enthusiasts can get wonderful photos of Irish Navy ships entering or leaving Haulbowline from the approach road to Cobh from Cork. Again there are photographic opportunities from the grounds and terrace of St. Colman's Cathedral, Cobh. The same locations can be used to capture car ferries to Britain and the Continent, but a better location is available from Whitepoint, midway between Cobh and Rushbrooke. An hourly train service operates from Cork to Carrigaloe, Rushbrooke and Cobh. Trains depart from Cork at 25 minutes past the hour, and from Cobh at 55 minutes past the hour.

The reclaimed area at Ringaskiddy is also a very good place to photograph the car ferries and all the many vessels which use Ringaskiddy deep water quay while the deepwater quay can be used itself, but permission should be requested from the entrance hut if ships are being worked at the quay. Ships in the channel leading to Cork City can be photographed from the old pier at Monkstown and from the roadways on either side of the river.

Ships of all types can be photographed traversing the port's entrance channel from the road leading to the former Military Fort at Camden near Crosshaven. This location requires the use of telephoto lens and photographers will need their own transport or else use the infrequent bus service to Crosshaven. Early morning arrivals and departures can be captured on film from Roche's Point itself but be warned as this location is at least 26 miles by road from Cork City centre - own transport is essential.

Above: The Carrigaloe-Glenbrook ferry has proved an overwhelming success since it was established in 1993. The *Carrigaloe*, one of the two vessels employed on the service. *(Jack Phelan)*
Below: Ferries of the Marine Transport at Cobh. *(Jack Phelan)*

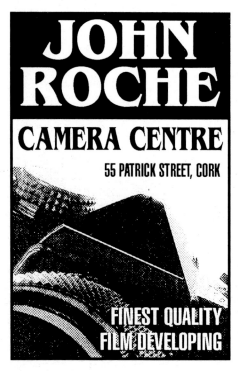

Ferry Publications was formed in 1988 by Miles Cowsill and John Hendy who had joined together to write and publish their highly successful *Townsend Thoresen Years*. Since then they have produced a continuous stream of titles which have covered most areas of the North Sea, English Channel and Irish Sea.

Disenchantment with writing for other magazines led the Partners to launch their own quarterly journal, *'British Ferry Scene'* in the Summer of 1989. Now a firmly established favourite, the magazine has quickly gained praise from both the enthusiast fraternity and the ferry industry alike.

For further information and details on current titles of Ferry Publications, please write to:
12 MILLFIELDS CLOSE,, KILGETTY, PEMBROKESHIRE, SA68 0SA.
TEL: (01834) 813991 FAX (01834) 814484